40

DAYS

— *of* —

GRACE

Books by Paul David Tripp

40 DAYS

—of—

GRACE

PAUL DAVID TRIPP

WHEATON, ILLINOIS

40 Days of Grace

Copyright © 2020 by Paul David Tripp

Published by Crossway
    1300 Crescent Street
    Wheaton, Illinois 60187

The devotions in this book appeared previously in Paul David Tripp, *New Morning Mercies: A Daily Gospel Devotional* (Wheaton, IL: Crossway, 2014).

Cover design: Josh Dennis

First printing, 2020

Printed in the United States of America

Trade paperback ISBN: 978-1-4335-7429-0
ePub ISBN: 978-1-4335-7432-0
PDF ISBN: 978-1-4335-7430-6
Mobipocket ISBN: 978-1-4335-7431-3

Library of Congress Cataloging-in-Publication Data

Names: Tripp, Paul David, 1950– author.
Title: 40 days of grace / Paul David Tripp.
Other titles: Forty days of grace
Description: Wheaton, Illinois: Crossway, 2020. | "The devotions in this book appeared previously in Paul David Tripp, New Morning Mercies: A Daily Gospel Devotional (Wheaton, IL: Crossway, 2014)."
Identifiers: LCCN 2020022784 | ISBN 9781433574290 (trade paperback) | ISBN 9781433574306 (pdf) | ISBN 9781433574313 (mobipocket) | ISBN 9781433574320 (epub)
Subjects: LCSH: Consolation—Meditations. | Grace (Theology)—Meditations.
Classification: LCC BV4905.3 .T686 2020 | DDC 242/.2—dc23
LC record available at https://lccn.loc.gov/2020022784

Crossway is a publishing ministry of Good News Publishers.

LB		28	27	26	25	24	23	22	
14	13	12	11	10	9	8	7	6	5	4	3	2

INTRODUCTION

GRACE IS A THUNDEROUS, expansive, powerful, and life-altering word. Other than the word *God*, there is no more important word that the human mind could consider and the mouth could speak. Grace is the ultimate spiritual game changer. It is the one thing that has the power to change you and everything about you. It is what all human beings need, no matter who they are or where they are. Men and women need grace, the young and old need grace, the rich and poor need grace, the popular and forgotten need grace, and the weak and powerful need grace. You could dig into grace every day of your life and not reach the bottom of its power and glory. Grace is the bottomless, treasure-laden mine of divine help. There simply is nothing comparable to God's amazing grace.

Grace explodes into your life in a moment, but will occupy you for all of eternity. It is the most transformational word in the Bible that you hold dear. In fact, your Bible is the cover-to-cover story of God's grace. It is the best of stories, the story of the undeserved redemption of lost ones and rebels. God's word records for us how God reached into the muck and mire of our sin-broken world to rescue us, not because of what he saw in us but because of what was in him. Grace is why God sent his Son into this world to do for us what we could not do for ourselves—to transform us from what we are (sinners separated from him) into what we are becoming (Christ-like and with him forever). John Newton, in his famous hymn, really did choose the best word ever to describe God's grace: *amazing*.

Grace is a wonderful story and the best gift ever. Grace is a jewel of God's character and the only reliable place to rest your hope. Grace is a tool that God uses to transform you, but it also defines the nature of his relationship to you. Because you are God's child, grace is something you'll never deserve but can always expect. Grace is a theology that you could study forever and the sweetest invitation you will ever receive. Grace will devastate you while giving you a peace of heart and a rest of soul you have never experienced before. Grace will require you to confess your unworthiness but will never, ever make you feel alone and unloved.

Grace will remind you again and again that you have no ability whatsoever to earn God's favor, but it will dispel your fear of not measuring up. Grace will confront you with the reality that you are way less than you thought you were while it comforts you with the promise that you can be way more than you ever imagined. Grace will repeatedly put you in your place but will never harm you by putting you down.

Grace will call you to examine yourself with honesty and humility, but will free you from being paralyzed by fearful introspection. God will ask you to admit to your catalog of weaknesses while at the same time empowering you with newfound strength. Grace will keep reminding you of what you are not so you will receive God's welcome to what you can now be. Yes, grace will drive you to the end of yourself while it holds before you the promise of fresh starts and new beginnings. Grace will blow up your little kingdom of one while it introduces you to a much better, more glorious King. Grace will work to expose your blindness while it gives you eyes to see. Grace will make you sadder than you have ever been in your life and give you cause for a joy and celebration that nothing or no one can take away. Grace is more than just a story, it's more than just a theology, and it's more than just a powerful force—no, grace is a person, and his name is Jesus. Jesus *is* the grace of God.

So I invite you to invest the next forty days in digging into the mine of God's grace with me. As we dig, pray for eyes that can see and a heart ready to receive the most wonderful, rescuing, forgiving, and transforming gift that has ever been given—God's amazing grace in the person of his Son, Jesus Christ.

DAY 1

*Face it, your most brilliant act of righteousness
wouldn't measure up to God's standard; that's
why you've been given the grace of Jesus.*

THE MORE YOU UNDERSTAND THE magnitude of God's grace, the more accurate will be your view of the depth of your unrighteousness; and the more you understand the depth of your unrighteousness, the more you will appreciate the magnitude of God's gift of grace. The person who is comfortable in his own righteousness hasn't really understood grace, and the person who is unimpressed by God's grace hasn't really understood his sin. So let's talk about the essentiality of God's grace.

To talk about the essential nature of God's grace means first talking about the disaster of sin. Sin isn't primarily about acts of rebellion. Sin is, first of all, a condition of the heart that results in acts of rebellion. You and I commit sins because we are sinners. The condition of sin, into which every person who has ever lived was born, renders each of us unable to live up to God's standard. Sin leaves us without the desire, will, or ability to do perfectly what God declares is right. Whether it's a situation in which we try and fail or a moment when we rebel and don't care, the playing field is level—we all fall short of God's standard. Read Romans 3. It is a devastating analysis that shows us all to be in a dire and unalterable spiritual condition. We are all unable, we are all guilty, and there is not a thing we can do to help ourselves. None of us is good in God's eyes and none of us can satisfy his requirement. It is an inescapable, humbling, and sad reality.

But God didn't leave us in this sorry, helpless, and hopeless state. He sent his Son to do what we could not do, to die as we should have died, and to rise again, defeating sin and death. He did all this so that we could rest in a righteousness that is not our own, but a righteousness that fully satisfies God's requirement. So, unable as we are, we are not without hope. We can stand before a perfectly holy God, broken, weak, and failing, and be completely unafraid because we stand before him in the righteousness of Jesus Christ. You no longer have to hope and pray that someday you will measure up, because Jesus has measured up on your behalf. How could you hear better news than that?

FOR FURTHER STUDY AND ENCOURAGEMENT
Galatians 3:15–29

DAY 2

*Grace has the power to do what nothing else
can do—rescue you from you, and in so doing,
restore you to what you were created to be.*

THEY'RE THE TWO ESSENTIAL PARTS of redemption, *rescue* and *restoration*, and you and I can't do either one for ourselves. But it's hard to admit that we have a problem that we cannot solve. We like to convince ourselves that our anger tells us more about the flawed people we live near than it tells us about ourselves. We like to think that our impatience is more about the poor planning or character of the people we have to deal with every day. We like to think that our sin can be blamed on the temptations of the fallen world around us. When we do or say what is wrong, we tend to point to a boss, a spouse, one of our children, a friend, a difficult situation, a busy day, the fact that we aren't feeling well, bad parents, some injustice, or a long catalog of other excuses. But the Bible is quite clear. We all suffer from the same terminal disease. None of us has escaped it. It's not caused by the people or situations around us. We brought this destroyer into the world with us. David says it this way: "Behold, I was brought forth in iniquity, and in sin did my mother conceive me" (Ps. 51:5).

You and I can try as we might to fool ourselves. We can work as we might to shrink from responsibility. We can develop skill at pointing the finger of blame to things around us. But there is simply no denying the harsh reality of the Bible's hard-to-accept message—we are our own biggest problem. We are the thing with which we need help. There is no greater danger than the danger we are to ourselves. We need help, help that we cannot give ourselves. We need help that is deeper than education, socialization, politics, or changes of relationship or location. If left on our own, we are doomed, "having no hope and without God in the world" (Eph. 2:12).

But the hope-infused story of Scripture is that we have not been left on our own. God has controlled the events of the world as part of his unstoppable agenda of *rescue* and *restoration*. He sent his holy Son to enter the world and suffer because of sin's mess. He sent him to live the perfect life that we would never live, to sacrifice himself on account of our sin, and to defeat the death that is sin's doom. It is an agenda of awesome grace extended to lost, rebellious, and self-excusing people, who even need that grace to understand how much they need that grace. This grace had to include rescue because we could not escape ourselves, and it had to include restoration because we had no power to transform ourselves into what he created and redeemed us to be. So today, confess your need. Denying it never leads anywhere good. Thank God for the rescue and restoration that is your hope. And determine to look honestly into the mirror of God's word so you will continue to remember how much you need what he has freely given.

FOR FURTHER STUDY AND ENCOURAGEMENT
Jeremiah 17:5–8

DAY 3

*I must remember that God didn't give me grace for my
kingdom to work, but to capture me for a better kingdom.*

IT WAS ONE OF THE SWEETEST, most precious things Jesus said
to his disciples. Remember, they were all really focused on "the
kingdom." Not that they were concerned about the honor of
the King or the success of his kingdom; no, what obsessed
them was their place in that kingdom. For them, the kingdom
was about personal power, prominence, and position. Do you
remember the incident recorded in Mark 9:30–37?

> They went on from there and passed through Galilee. And
> he did not want anyone to know, for he was teaching his
> disciples, saying to them, "The Son of Man is going to be
> delivered into the hands of men, and they will kill him.
> And when he is killed, after three days he will rise." But they
> did not understand the saying, and were afraid to ask him.
> And they came to Capernaum. And when he was in the
> house he asked them, "What were you discussing on the
> way?" But they kept silent, for on the way they had argued
> with one another about who was the greatest. And he sat
> down and called the twelve. And he said to them, "If anyone
> would be first, he must be last of all and servant of all." And
> he took a child and put him in the midst of them, and taking
> him in his arms, he said to them, "Whoever receives one
> such child in my name receives me, and whoever receives
> me, receives not me but him who sent me."

Right after Jesus told them that he was going to be captured and killed, they didn't say: "Lord, no, no, you can't let this happen. What will we do without you?" They weren't filled with remorse. No, they began fighting with one another about which one of them was the greatest. This is what sin does to all of us. It causes us all to be little self-sovereigns and self-appointed mini-kings. What we really want is for *our* kingdoms to come and our will to be done right here, right now in our jobs and families. We love being in control. We love getting our own way. We love being indulged and served. We live for being right. We have a wonderful plan for the people in our lives. It is humbling to admit, but we are more like the disciples than unlike them.

So it was a moment of beautiful grace when Jesus looked at these self-oriented disciples and said, "Fear not, little flock, for it is your Father's good pleasure to give you the kingdom" (Luke 12:32). He was saying: "Don't you understand? I didn't come to exercise my power to make your little kingdoms work, but to welcome you, by grace, to a much better kingdom than you could ever quest for on your own." No matter how counterintuitive it is, it really is true that real life is found only when his kingdom comes and his will is done, and that is exactly what grace welcomes you to.

FOR FURTHER STUDY AND ENCOURAGEMENT
Matthew 13:44–50

DAY 4

God's grace will expose what you want to hide,
not to shame you, but to forgive and deliver you.

"IT'S A SAD WAY TO LIVE," I thought as I listened to him recount the events of the night before. He worked next to me on the long packing table that kept our hands busy eight hours a day. But our mouths were free to talk, and talk we did. He was being unfaithful to his wife. He thought he was in charge, he thought he was free, but he wasn't. He told of taking his girlfriend to a certain restaurant in the small community where he lived, only to see his wife's car parked outside. He told of going to another place but having to make sure the coast was clear before they left so they wouldn't get caught. I said to him: "You think you're free, but you're not free. You have to hide. You have to worry about being caught. You have to lurk around in the darkness." I then said: "You think I'm bound, but I'm the one who's free. When I go out with my wife, I never have to worry about where we're going. I never have to fear being caught. I can boldly live in the light."

Sin turns all of us into citizens of the night. Sin causes all of us to be committed to low-light living. We hide, we deny, we cover, we lie, we excuse, we shift the blame, we rationalize, we defend, and we explain away. These are all acts of darkness by people who fear exposure.

What is the movement of grace? It is to shine light on what once lived in darkness. "And this is the judgment: the light has come into the world, and people loved the darkness rather than the light because their deeds were evil. For everyone who does wicked things hates the light and does not come to the light, lest his works should be exposed" (John 3:19–20). Grace shatters our darkness. Grace explodes on us with penetrating, heart-exposing light. Grace illumines our dank hallways and our dark corners. The Son of grace shines the light of his grace into the darkest recesses of our hearts, not as an act of vengeance or punishment, but as a move of forgiving, transforming, and delivering grace. He dispels our self-inflicted darkness because he knows that we cannot grieve what we do not see, we cannot confess what we have not grieved, and we cannot turn from what we haven't confessed.

The light has come. Run to the light; it is not to be feared. Yes, it is the light of exposure, but what will be exposed has already been covered by the blood of the one who exposes it.

FOR FURTHER STUDY AND ENCOURAGEMENT

John 1:1–18

DAY 5

*Quit being paralyzed by your past. Grace offers you
life in the present and the guarantee of a future.*

IT IS A SIMPLE FACT OF NATURE that once the leaves are off the tree, you cannot put them back again. Once you have uttered words, you cannot rip them out of another's hearing. Once you have acted on a choice, you cannot relive that moment again. Once you have behaved in a certain way at a certain time, you cannot ask for a redo. You and I just don't have the option of reliving our past to try to do better any more than we have the power to glue the leaves back on the tree and make them live once again. What's done is done and cannot be redone.

But we all wish we could live certain moments and certain decisions over again. If you're at all humble and able to look back on your past with a degree of accuracy, you experience regret. None of us has always desired the right thing. None of us has always made the best decision. None of us has always been humble, kind, and loving. We haven't always jumped to serve and forgive. None of us has always spoken the truth. None of us has been free of anger, envy, or vengeance. None of us has walked through life with unblemished nobility. None of us. So all of us have reason for remorse and regret. All of us are left with the sadness of what has been done and can't be undone.

That's why all of us should daily celebrate the grace that frees us from the regret of the past. This freedom is not the freedom of retraction or denial. It's not the freedom of rewriting our history. No, it's the freedom of forgiving and transforming grace. This grace welcomes me to live with hope in the present because it frees me to leave my past behind. All of what I look back on and would like to redo has been fully covered by the blood of Jesus. I no longer need to carry the burden of the past on my shoulders, so I am free to fully give myself to what God has called me to in the here and now. "But one thing I do: forgetting what lies behind and straining forward to what lies ahead, I press on toward the goal for the prize of the upward call of God in Christ Jesus" (Phil. 3:13–14).

Are you paralyzed by your past? Are you living under the dark shroud of the "if-onlys"? Does your past influence your present more than God's past, present, and future grace? Have you received and are you living out of the forgiveness that is yours because of the life, death, and resurrection of Jesus?

FOR FURTHER STUDY AND ENCOURAGEMENT

Jeremiah 29:1–14

DAY 6

*It would be amazing if a God of awesome glory
recognized our existence, but for him to welcome
us into his family is grace beyond amazing!*

IT IS JUST SO INCREDIBLE, so counterintuitive, and so beyond anything else in our experience that it is very hard for us to wrap our brains around its majesty. There is no human being so creative and imaginative as to be able to pen such a story. You can read the story in Scripture and still not be blown away by its glory because you just don't have categories to understand its depth and breadth. In fact, it takes what this story is about for you to fully understand what this story is about. Only the gift of divine grace is able to help you grasp even a portion of the wonder of divine grace. The expansiveness of God's initiative of grace is so beautiful and transformational that it is the reason John Newton chose the best qualifying word, *amazing*, when he penned his famous hymn about that grace.

Think about it. No human being ever kept God's law (except Jesus). No one has ever given God the honor due his name. No one has lived the life of worship that is the duty and calling of everyone who has ever taken a breath. All people have not only rebelled against God, but they have written their own sets of self-oriented rules. Everyone not only has failed to worship God, but also has worshiped false gods. Every human being not only has failed to recognize the centrality of God in all things, but also has inserted himself or herself in God's position. Everyone not only occasionally breaks one or another of God's laws, but we all, in some way, have broken all of his laws. Not only do we misuse God's creation, but we put it in God's place and give it the worship that belongs to him.

So in the face of the depth and heinous character of all of our rebellion against God and his glory, it would be amazing if we were not exterminated. It would be an act of wondrous grace for God to recognize that we exist. But he has done so much, much more than this. By means of the life, death, and resurrection of his Son, he has made a way for us to be welcomed into an intimate familial relationship with him. He literally adopts us into his family so that, quite apart from anything we could have ever deserved, we are given the full range of rights and privileges of his children. And not only are we granted those things in the here and now, but we are blessed with them forever and ever. Along with this, he has promised us the final end of all the sin, sickness, sorrow, and suffering that our rebellion brought down on this world. So grace lets you have it all—everything, that is, that you need. Grace makes the King of kings your Father and his Savior Son your brother. Now, that really is beyond amazing. Pray for eyes to see it and a heart to embrace it, and then let your soul soar.

FOR FURTHER STUDY AND ENCOURAGEMENT
Ephesians 1:15–23

DAY 7

You don't get wisdom by experience or research.
You get wisdom by means of relationship.
Grace makes that relationship possible.

IT IS ONE OF THE OFTEN UNDERSTATED, definitively dark, and dangerous results of sin. What is it? Sin reduces all of us to fools. Sadly, we demonstrate that foolishness every day. We think we can spend what we want to satisfy our seemingly endless desires without getting into hopeless debt. We think that sex, food, and fun will satisfy the hunger of our hearts for contentment and life. We think we can rebel against authority, and it will be all right in the end. We think we can be selfish and demanding in our relationships, and our loved ones will still want to be near us. We think we can pursue the pleasures of creation at any time and in any way we want, and not get fat, addicted, and in debt. We think that we can step over God's boundaries without consequences. We think we deserve what we do not deserve and are able to do what we cannot do. Shockingly, there are more times than most of us recognize or would be willing to admit when we think we're smarter than God.

To sinners (and that includes us all), wisdom is not natural. It is one of humanity's most profoundly important quests. Perhaps there are few more significant questions than this: "Where is wisdom to be found?" It is hard for us to gain wisdom by research or experience because they are filtered and interpreted by our own foolish hearts! It is here that the Bible greets us with a radical, counterintuitive message. You can't buy wisdom. You can't get it by hard work or lots of experience. No, wisdom is the result of *rescue* and *relationship*. To be wise, you first need to be rescued from you. You need to be given a new heart, one that is needy, humble, seeking, and ready to get from above what you can't find on this earth. And then you need to be brought into a relationship with the one who *is* wisdom. Colossians 2:3 says of Jesus, "in [him] are hidden all the treasures of wisdom and knowledge." Think of this: grace has connected you to the one who is wisdom. Grace has caused wisdom to live inside you. This means that wisdom is always with you and is always available to you.

The one who is wisdom now guides you. Wisdom protects you. Wisdom convicts you. Wisdom teaches and matures you. Wisdom encourages and comforts you. Wisdom works to change your thoughts and redirect your desires. Wisdom forgives your past and holds your future in his hands. And wisdom will welcome you into an eternity where foolishness will be no more. Today you will once again demonstrate your need for wisdom's work. Don't resist. Reach out for help with a thankful heart; wisdom has come to be with you forever.

FOR FURTHER STUDY AND ENCOURAGEMENT
Proverbs 2

DAY 8

Grace doesn't help you just to do different things
but to become a totally different person by
changing you at the level of your heart.

I WANT TO REFER YOU RIGHT NOW to one of the Bible's best-known prayers of confession. The problem is that it's so familiar to most of us that we've quit giving it the examination that it requires in order for us to receive from it the rescue that it offers. The confession is David's in Psalm 51:1–12:

Have mercy on me, O God,
    according to your steadfast love;
according to your abundant mercy
    blot out my transgressions.
Wash me thoroughly from my iniquity,
    and cleanse me from my sin!

For I know my transgressions,
    and my sin is ever before me.
Against you, you only, have I sinned
    and done what is evil in your sight,
so that you may be justified in your words
    and blameless in your judgment.
Behold, I was brought forth in iniquity,
    and in sin did my mother conceive me.
Behold, you delight in truth in the inward being,
    and you teach me wisdom in the secret heart.

Purge me with hyssop, and I shall be clean;
    wash me, and I shall be whiter than snow.
Let me hear joy and gladness;
    let the bones that you have broken rejoice.
Hide your face from my sins,
    and blot out all my iniquities.
Create in me a clean heart, O God,
    and renew a right spirit within me.
Cast me not away from your presence,
    and take not your Holy Spirit from me.
Restore to me the joy of your salvation,
    and uphold me with a willing spirit.

Look carefully at the words of David's prayer. This is not only a prayer of confession—it is also a cry for change. He admits that his problem is not environmental, but natal; he came into the world with it. He confesses that his problem is not external, but internal; it's a problem of the "inward being." So he cries out for what every sinner needs: a new heart. It is something only God can create. It is the epicenter of his work of grace. He wants more than reformed behavior; he sent his Son to die for you so that you would have a new heart, one that is constantly being renewed. If your heart is your problem, then the grace of heart change is your only hope.

FOR FURTHER STUDY AND ENCOURAGEMENT
Matthew 15:10–20

DAY 9

We are guilty. The cross purchased our forgiveness.
We are unable. The Spirit gives us power.
We are foolish. God's word provides wisdom.

What did I bring
to your salvation table?
I had
no righteousness to offer,
no strength to give,
no wisdom to present.
There was
nothing
that I could deliver
that would commend me
to you.
I crawled broken
to your table,
weighed down and crippled by
my sin,
my guilt,
my weakness,
my foolishness,
my pride,
my shame.

I had no right
to be with you,
but you picked me up
and placed me there.
You fed me
the life-giving nutrients
of grace
with your
nail-scarred hands.
And I haven't left your
table of mercy since.

FOR FURTHER STUDY AND ENCOURAGEMENT

Romans 8:18–30

DAY 10

*For sin, forgiveness; for weakness, strength; for
foolishness, wisdom; for bondage, deliverance—
such is the way of the grace of Jesus.*

I LOVE COLOSSIANS 2 (stop now and read verses 1–15). Maybe I love it so much because Luella, my wife, is the owner and director of a large private art gallery. You might be thinking, "Well, that's a strange comment, Paul." Permit me to explain. Colossians 2:1–15 is like a gallery of God's grace.

At the beginning of each month, artwork is delivered to Luella's gallery for the next show. The paintings come wrapped protectively or boxed in crates, and it is exciting for Luella to open them and to begin to experience the art that will give life to the gallery over the next month. After she has unpacked all the artwork, Luella goes through the process of arranging and rearranging it until each piece is where it needs to be to be displayed with the most power. The next day, a team of hangers comes into the gallery to help Luella actually affix the paintings to the walls. The final step is for each painting to be properly lit. Every month, it seems that the gallery actually changes shape with the new work. Once it's lit, I like to come down to the gallery in the evening and see the work in all its splendor. Often Luella and I stand across the street at night, look into the huge gallery windows, and take in the beauty. Then Luella does something that bothers me every time. She gets her briefcase and hits the light switch, plunging the gallery into darkness. I always think, "No, no, these paintings should never be in the dark."

If you're God's child, you are a gallery of his glorious grace. The walls of your heart have been festooned with the gorgeous artwork of redemption: wisdom for the foolishness of sin, power for the weakness of sin, forgiveness for the guilt of sin, and deliverance from the bondage of sin. Grace means that beautiful things are being done for you and happening within you. Yet I have this concern—for many believers, the artwork is there, but the lights are out in the gallery. These believers simply don't see or fully understand the stunning beauty of what they have been given in the grace of the Lord Jesus Christ. And because they don't see or understand that grace, they neither celebrate it nor live in light of its majesty. So they give way to weakness when power is at their disposal. They give way to foolishness when they have been personally connected to the one who is wisdom. They hide in guilt when they have been fully forgiven. They surrender to addiction when they have been given freeing grace. Their hearts have been decorated with the artwork of grace, but the lights are out in the gallery. How sad! What about you? Are the lights on, and has that radically changed the way you live?

FOR FURTHER STUDY AND ENCOURAGEMENT
Galatians 5:16–26

DAY 11

*If you are God's child, you're either giving in to
sin or giving way to the operation of rescuing
grace, but your heart's never neutral.*

ONE OF THE BEAUTIFUL RESULTS of God's redeeming grace in
your life and mine is that the hearts of stone have been taken
out of us and replaced with hearts of flesh. Think of the word
picture here. If I had a stone in my hands and I pressed it with
all of my might, what do you think would happen? Well, if you
could see the size of my arms, you would immediately know
the answer to the question. I could press that stone with all of
the strength that I have and nothing whatsoever would happen. Stone is not malleable. It exists in a fixed shape. Before
your conversion, you had that kind of heart. It was resistant
to change. But that is not true any longer. Grace has given
you a fleshy heart, one that is moldable by transforming grace.

Now, this means that when you sin, desiring, thinking,
saying, or doing what is wrong in God's eyes, your conscience
bothers you. What we're talking about here is the convicting
ministry of the Holy Spirit. When your conscience bothers
you, you have only two choices. You can gladly confess that
what you've done is sin and place yourself once again under the
justifying mercies of Christ, or you can erect some system of
self-justification that makes what God says is wrong acceptable
to your conscience. We are all so good at doing this. We are
good at pointing to something or someone who justifies what

we have done. We are all very good at systems of self-atonement that essentially argue for our righteousness.

What is deadly about this is that when you convince yourself that you are righteous, you quit seeking the grace that is your only hope in life or death. "If we say we have no sin, we deceive ourselves, and the truth is not in us. If we confess our sins, he is faithful and just to forgive us our sins and to cleanse us from all unrighteousness" (1 John 1:8–9).

The fact of the matter is that none of us are grace graduates, including the man who is writing this devotion. We are all in daily and desperate need of forgiving, rescuing, transforming, and delivering grace. When you resist humble acknowledgment of your sin, you resist the ever-present Redeemer who is making that sin known to you. He does this not to humiliate or punish you, but because he loves you so much that he will not turn from his work of grace in your heart until that work has accomplished all that Jesus died to give you. There is little room for neutrality here. Today you will resist grace or you will humbly run to grace. May the latter be your choice.

FOR FURTHER STUDY AND ENCOURAGEMENT
Galatians 6:1–10

DAY 12

*Confession is a grace. Only grace can convince
you to abandon your righteousness and run
to the merciful arms of the Lord.*

CONFESSION IS NOT NATURAL FOR US. It's natural for us to think of ourselves as more righteous than we are. It's natural to blame our wrongs on others. It's natural to say our behavior was caused by some difficult circumstance we were in. It's natural to exercise our inner lawyers and defend ourselves when we're confronted with a sin, weakness, or failure. It's natural to turn the tables when being confronted and tell our accusers that they are surely bigger sinners than we are. It's natural to see ourselves more as law keepers than as lawbreakers. It's natural to point to our biblical literacy or theological knowledge as proof of our spiritual maturity. It's natural to be more concerned about the sin of others than our own. It's natural to be more critical of the attitudes and behavior of others than our own. It's natural for you and me to be blind to the depth of our spiritual need.

Because this sturdy system of self-righteousness is natural for every sinner, it is unnatural for us to be clear-sighted, humble, self-examining, and ready to confess. Blind eyes and a self-satisfied, self-congratulatory heart stand in the way of the broken heart of confession. We don't grieve our sin because we don't see it. It is ironic that we tend to see the righteousness we don't have and we fail to see the sin that stains every day of our lives.

Here's how confession works. You cannot *confess* what you haven't *grieved*, you can't *grieve* what you do not *see*, and you cannot *repent of* what you have not *confessed*. So one of the most important operations of God's grace is to give us eyes to see our sin and hearts that are willing to confess it. If your eyes are open and you see yourself with accuracy, and if your heart is humbly willing to admit to what your eyes see, you know that glorious, rescuing, forgiving, and transforming grace has visited you. Why? Because what you're doing is simply not natural for sinners. In the face of their sin, Adam blamed Eve, Eve blamed the serpent, and both of them hid, but neither stepped forward and made willing and heartfelt confession.

So cry out today for eyes to see, that is, for accurate personal insight. Cry out for the defenses of your heart to come down. Ask God to defeat your fear of being exposed, of being known. Cry for the grace to be willing to stop, look, listen, receive, grieve, confess, and turn. Stand with courage and hope before the searching and exposing mirror of the word of God, and be unafraid. Stand naked before God and know that all that is exposed has been fully and completely covered by the shed blood of your Savior. Because of him, you don't need to be afraid of your unrighteousness; no, it is your delusions of righteousness that are the grave danger.

FOR FURTHER STUDY AND ENCOURAGEMENT

Acts 3:11–26

DAY 13

*God's grace calls you to submit. But it offers you
true freedom like you've never known before.*

I THINK WE MISUNDERSTAND both true freedom and debili-
tating bondage. Freedom that fills and satisfies your heart
is never found in setting yourself up as your own authority.
True freedom is not found in doing whatever you want to do
whenever you want to do it. True freedom is never found in
putting yourself in the middle of your world and making it all
about you. True freedom is not found in resisting the call to
submit to any authority but your own. True freedom is never
found in writing your own moral code. True freedom is not
the result of finally getting your own way. When you attempt
to do these things, you never enjoy freedom; you only end up
in another form of bondage.

Why is this true? It's true because you and I were born into
a world of authority. First, there is the overarching authority
of God. There is nothing that exists that does not sit under
his sovereign and unshakable rule. If God created this world
(and he did) and if he owns what he created (and he does),
then you and I do not have autonomy (independence from his
rule). This means that as his creatures, we were created to live
in willing submission to his will for us. Hence, freedom is not
found in spinning free of his authority. No, freedom is found
in the willing submission of our hearts to his authority. Then
there are all the levels of human authority that God put on

earth to make his invisible authority visible. Personal freedom is not found in resisting human authority either. Freedom and authority are not enemies.

Here is the point: you and I always exist under some kind of authority. We either willingly submit to God's rule and the authorities that he has placed in our lives or we set ourselves up as our own authorities and rule our lives as we see fit. But none of us is wise enough, strong enough, faithful enough, or righteous enough to rule ourselves well. We are no more hardwired to rule our own lives than a beagle is hardwired to live in a water-filled aquarium. Self-rule never leads anywhere good.

So the goal of grace is not to produce in you the ability to live independently. The agenda of grace is to transform you into a person who humbly recognizes your need for authority and celebrates the holy, loving, and benevolent authority of God. "But now that you have been set free from sin and have become slaves of God, the fruit you get leads to sanctification and its end, eternal life" (Rom. 6:22). It is sin that makes me want to rule myself and it is grace that draws me into the only slavery that gives life, slavery to the Creator, the Savior King who knows what is best and gives what is best always.

FOR FURTHER STUDY AND ENCOURAGEMENT
Romans 13:1–7

DAY 14

Fish were designed to swim, the sun to shine, and
you to worship God. Grace welcomes you back
to what you were designed for—worship.

IF SOMEONE WERE TO ASK YOU what the ultimate, final goal of God's grace is, what would you answer? What is God's grace working to accomplish? God's grace can make you more financially wise. God's grace can make you a better citizen and neighbor. God's grace can cause you to be more responsible with the use of your body and more sexually pure. God's grace can help you to make better decisions in life. God's grace can assist you to communicate in a way that is less selfish and more loving toward others. God's grace can help you to think more about the future and rescue you from living just for the here and now. God's grace can make you more thankful and a better steward of what you have been given. God's grace can cause you to be a wiser and more patient parent. God's grace can help you to forge a healthier marriage. God's grace can enable you to be more honest with yourself and more forgiving in your dealings with others. God's grace can make you less anxious and more courageous. God's grace can give you a reason to get up in the morning even when things aren't going well. God's grace can pilot you through disappointment and give you joy even when you're suffering. God's grace can enable you to remember what is worth remembering and to put away what you need to forget. God's grace can make you more compassionate and less bitter. God's grace can help you to know you are loved even when you're alone and to know you have strength even when you are weak. All of these things are the beautiful harvest of grace. All of these are things for which we should be eternally thankful. But none of these good gifts is the ultimate goal of God's grace. Focus on the following words from Romans 1:18–23:

> For the wrath of God is revealed from heaven against all ungodliness and unrighteousness of men, who by their unrighteousness suppress the truth. For what can be known about God is plain to them, because God has shown it to them. For his invisible attributes, namely, his eternal power and divine nature, have been clearly perceived, ever since the creation of the world, in the things that have been made. So they are without excuse. For although they knew God, they did not honor him as God or give thanks to him, but they became futile in their thinking, and their foolish hearts were darkened. Claiming to be wise, they became fools, and exchanged the glory of the immortal God for images resembling mortal man and birds and animals and creeping things.

Sin kidnapped our worship, and grace works to restore it to its rightful owner—God. Only when God is in his rightful place in our hearts is everything else in its appropriate place in our lives, and only powerful grace can accomplish this.

FOR FURTHER STUDY AND ENCOURAGEMENT
Deuteronomy 10:12–22

DAY 15

Grace frees you from the dissatisfying claustrophobia
of your individualism to enjoy the fulfilling
freedom of loving and serving God.

INDIVIDUALISM IS NOT FREEDOM; it is bondage. Living for
yourself is not liberty; it is a self-imposed prison. Doing what
you want to do, when you want to do it, and how you want
to do it has never been the good life; it never leads to anything
good. Making up your own rules and following your own paths
leads to disaster. God calls you to himself and commands you
to follow him so that, by grace, he may free you from you. In
calling you to obedience, God is not robbing you of liberty,
but is leading you to the only place where liberty can be found.

To understand this, you must look at life from the vantage
point of creation and the fall into sin. As Creator, God designed you to live a dependent life. You were built for a life
of loving, worshipful dependency and obedience. You and I
just don't have the power and wisdom we would need to live
an independent existence. To try to live life completely independent of God is like trying to drive a beautiful boat down a
superhighway. That boat is a wonderful creation, loaded with
amazing design details, but it was not built to run on a hard
surface. If you try to run it on land, you will destroy the boat
and you will go nowhere fast.

The entrance of sin into the world and into our hearts
teaches us that we were not hardwired for independence. It

also complicated things. The fall made us all a danger to ourselves. Because of the sin in us, we think bad things, we desire bad things, we are attracted to bad things, and we choose bad things—and we are blind to much of this going on inside of ourselves. So not only do we need God's presence and his wisdom to guide and protect us, but we also need his grace to rescue us.

The doctrines of creation and the fall drive us to conclude that living for ourselves—that is, working to independently rule our own little worlds—can never work. Life is only ever found when we put ourselves in the hands of our Creator and cast ourselves on his amazing grace. An honest look at how you were put together by the Creator and at what sin did to you destroys any confidence you have in your ability to make it on your own and drives you to the cross of the Lord Jesus Christ.

It really is true that individualism is a delusion, that joyful submission is the good life, and that Jesus alone is able to transport you from one to the other. If you find more joy in serving God than yourself, you know that grace has entered your door, because only grace has the power to rescue you from you.

FOR FURTHER STUDY AND ENCOURAGEMENT
John 8:31–38

DAY 16

*For the believer, obedience is not a pain but
a joy. Each act of obedience celebrates the
grace that motivates and empowers it.*

I REMEMBER MY BROTHER TEDD saying it to me, but I didn't
realize how right he was: "Obedience is its own reward." It
is hard to overestimate the grace that motivates each act of
obedience in your life and in mine:

- Sinners tend not to esteem authority.
- Sinners like to write their own rules.
- Sinners are good at convincing themselves that their
  wrongs are not that wrong.
- Sinners tend to believe in their own autonomy.
- Sinners tend to think they're wiser than they are.
- Sinners tend to have a moral code that is formed more
  by their desires than by God's law.
- Sinners tend to think that they don't need what they
  don't desire.
- Sinners tend to be self-focused and self-excusing.
- Sinners tend to crave what God has prohibited.
- Sinners tend to opt for short-term pleasure over long-
  term gain.
- Sinners tend to rebel rather than submit.

Because all of the above statements are true, it is a miracle
of amazing grace that any of us ever chooses to obey God. It is

even more a miracle that we can find joy in obeying someone whom we cannot see, hear, or touch. It is a wonder of transforming grace that the heart of a self-focused human being can abandon the pursuit of his own little kingdom and give itself to serve the purposes of the kingdom of another. Any time we desire, in word, thought, or action, to do what pleases God, we are being rescued, transformed, and empowered by his grace. You see, your obedience celebrates grace even in moments when you aren't consciously celebrating it yourself. Each moment of submission to the will of God celebrates this reality: "For sin will have no dominion over you, since you are not under law but under grace" (Rom. 6:14).

So smile when you obey; you are experiencing the riches of grace. Give thanks when you submit; you are being rescued by grace. Celebrate when you make the right choice; you are being transformed by grace. Sing for joy when you serve God's purposes; you have just given evidence of the presence of redeeming grace!

FOR FURTHER STUDY AND ENCOURAGEMENT
1 Corinthians 6:1–11

DAY 17

While sin is still a sad and ever-present reality
in each of our lives, it is simply no match
for the grace of the Lord Jesus Christ.

ONE OF THE THEMES of this devotional is that biblical faith never requires that you deny reality. If you have to turn your back on what is real and true in order to have some temporary personal peace, you may feel better, but what you're exercising is not the faith of the Bible. This realism applies to the sin that still remains in you and is being progressively eradicated by God's powerful grace. There is a great temptation to deny or at least to minimize our sin. However, you are never moving in a productive spiritual direction when, by self-atoning arguments, you make your sin look less like sin. You don't protect the message of the gospel by denying your own spiritual struggles, and God surely doesn't need you to defend his reputation by faking it.

This is not to say you should make your sin the focus of your meditation. It is simply a denial of the amazing grace of the gospel of Jesus Christ to treat yourself as an unworthy, impure, and incapable spiritual worm. You must not meditate on the judgment of God. You must not squirm at the thought of his presence. You must not allow yourself to wonder if he loves you. You must not see yourself as unworthy of his care. You must not work to measure up in his sight. You must not think that he acts more favorably to you when you are obedient than when you sin. You must not beat yourself up when you fail. You must not give yourself to acts of payment and penance after you have messed up in God's eyes. You must not envy the worthiness of the person next to you, as if he or she is more accepted by God because he or she is more spiritually mature than you. You must never run from God in fear as you think of the empirical evidence of remaining sin that you give every day.

What you and I must meditate on every day is the absolute perfection and completeness of the work of the Lord Jesus Christ. He was perfect in his life, perfect in his death, and perfect in his resurrection. There is nothing we could ever think, desire, say, or do that could in any way add to the forgiveness and acceptance that we have received from God based on Christ's work. You are perfect in the eyes of God because the perfect righteousness of Jesus has been attributed to your spiritual account. You are righteous before God even in those moments when what you are doing is not righteous. You measure up in his eyes even on those days when you don't measure up, because Jesus measured up on your behalf. Yes, you should acknowledge the sad reality of remaining sin, but you must not make that sin your meditation. Meditate on and celebrate the amazing grace that has completely changed your identity, potential, and destiny.

FOR FURTHER STUDY AND ENCOURAGEMENT
Galatians 3:1–14

DAY 18

God's grace not only provides you with
what you need, but also transforms you into
what he in wisdom created you to be.

WHAT IS IT THAT YOU NEED MOST? No, it's not that girl or that new car that you've had your eyes on. It's not that promotion you've worked so hard for or that vacation you've dreamed of. No, it's not the perseverance to lose the weight you know you need to lose or the discipline to climb your way out of debt. It's not a closer circle of friends or a solid church to attend. It's not freedom from physical sickness or restoration to your estranged family. It's not freedom from addiction, fear, depression, or worry. All of these things are very important in their own way, but they don't represent your biggest need. There is one thing that every human being desperately needs, whether he knows it or not. This need gets to the heart of who you are and the heart of what God designed you to be and to do.

Your biggest need (and mine) is a fully restored relationship with God. We were created to live in worshipful community with him. Our lives were meant to be shaped by love for him. We were hardwired to live for his glory. If you are still living in a broken relationship to him, you are missing the primary purpose for your existence. So God in grace made a way, through the life, death, and resurrection of his Son, for that essential relationship to be fully restored. Through him, we are once again given access to the Father. Through him, we are restored to God's family.

But God does even more than this. As great as is the miracle that sinners, by grace, can be restored to God, he knows that there is something else that must be addressed. Sin not only left us separated from God, it left us damaged too. The damage of sin extends to every aspect of our personhood. So God not only meets our deepest need, he commits himself to the long-term process of personal heart and life transformation. He is not satisfied that we have been restored to him; he now works that we will become like him. Paul says it this way: "For those whom he foreknew he also predestined to be conformed to the image of his Son" (Rom. 8:29).

So God has welcomed you into his arms, but he's not satisfied. He will not leave his work of redemption until every heart of every one of his children has been fully transformed by his powerful grace. Now that we are *with* him by grace, he works by the very same grace that we will be *like* him.

FOR FURTHER STUDY AND ENCOURAGEMENT

2 Peter 1:3–11

DAY 19

*If you have quit being defensive and are now
willingly and humbly approachable, you know
that transforming grace has visited you.*

IT STARTED IN THE GARDEN OF EDEN, and we have been committed to it ever since. We all point the finger of blame and we all work to convince ourselves that the party to blame is not us. Adam pointed his finger at Eve, and Eve pointed her finger at the serpent; neither one of them accepted blame. Yes, it is true: there have been generations and generations of finger pointers ever since.

You see, when you've done something wrong, it's not natural to look inside yourself for the cause. Sin makes us all shockingly self-righteous. It makes us all committed self-excusers. Somehow, some way, we all buy into the delusion that our biggest problems live outside us, not inside us. We all have very active inner lawyers, who rise to our defense in the face of any accusation of wrong. We are all very skilled at presenting the logic of the argument that what we have done says more about the flawed people and dysfunctional things around us than it does about us. When our consciences bother us because of the faithful convicting ministry of the Holy Spirit, we are all tempted to dodge blame by locating the cause elsewhere. We all tend to be much more concerned about the sin of others than we are about our own, but, John says, "If we say we have no sin, we deceive ourselves, and the truth is not in us" (1 John 1:8).

Because accepting blame is not natural, it takes rescuing, transforming grace to produce a humble, willing, broken, self-examining, help-seeking heart. Only divine grace can soften a person's heart. Only grace can help your eyes to see what you need to see. Only grace can decimate your defenses and lead you to confess. Only grace can cause you to quit pointing your finger and to run to your Redeemer for his forgiveness and delivering power. Only grace can enable you to forsake your own righteousness and find your hope and rest in the righteousness of another. Only grace can make you more grieved over your sin than about the sins of others. Only grace can make you accept your need for grace. Only grace can cause you and me to abandon our confidence in our own performance and place our confidence in the perfectly acceptable righteousness of Jesus Christ. Only grace can cause us to put our hope in the only place where hope can be found—in God and God alone. Every moment of defensiveness argues how much grace is still needed.

FOR FURTHER STUDY AND ENCOURAGEMENT
1 John 1:5–10

DAY 20

*Grace doesn't make it okay for you to live
for you. No, grace frees you to experience the
joy of living for one greater than you.*

IT IS UNIVERSALLY TRUE that what seems to us to be freedom isn't really freedom after all. When Adam and Eve stepped outside of God's boundaries, they didn't step into freedom. They stepped into toil, temptation, suffering, sin, and bondage. Denying God's existence, desiring his place, ignoring his rules, and determining to make it on your own might seem like pathways to freedom, but they never, ever are.

You and I weren't designed to live independently. We weren't meant to live in our own strength. We weren't created to rely on our own wisdom. We weren't given the ability to write our own moral codes. We weren't put together with the independent knowledge of how to live, how to steward the physical world, or how to properly relate to one another. We were not created to live *by* ourselves or *for* ourselves, and to attempt to do so never leads anywhere good.

So as God blesses us and changes us with his grace, the result isn't a greater ability to live an independent life; the opposite is true. Grace doesn't free us to live for us. The purpose of God's grace is not to make your little kingdom of one work better. The purpose of God's grace is to free you from your slavery to you so that you can live for a much, much better kingdom: "And he died for all, that those who live might no longer live for themselves but for him who for their sake died and was raised" (2 Cor. 5:15). True freedom is never found in putting yourself at the center, with your choices and behavior shaped by your allegiance to you. Real freedom is only ever found when God's grace liberates you to live for one infinitely greater than you.

It contradicts our normal thinking, but the doorway to freedom is submission. When I acknowledge that I am a danger to myself and submit to the authority, wisdom, and grace of God, I am not killing any hope I have for freedom. The opposite is true. Humble admission of need and humble submission to God open me up to the freest of lives. I was created to live in worshipful and obedient dependency on God, and when grace restores me to that place, it also gives me back my freedom. It may seem constricting that the train always has to ride on those tracks, but try driving it in a meadow and all motion stops. So grace puts you back on the tracks again and gives you the freedom of forward motion, which you can have no other way.

FOR FURTHER STUDY AND ENCOURAGEMENT
Romans 6:1–14

DAY 21

The grace you've been given is not just the grace
of forgiveness and acceptance; it's also the grace
of empowerment. So get up and follow.

IN THE LIFE OF THE BELIEVER, fear of weakness amounts to God-forgetfulness. Timidity is a failure to remember the promises of the gospel. Allowing yourself to be overwhelmed in the face of the call of God is forgetting the right here, right now grace of Jesus Christ. Giving way to temptation is overlooking the empowering presence of the Holy Spirit. You not only have been forgiven by the grace of the gospel and guaranteed a place in eternity with your Savior, but you also have been granted by that very same grace all that you need to be what God has called you to be and to do the things God has called you to do in the place where he has put you.

So here's how this works. God has promised to supply and empower; your job is to follow him by faith where you live every day. You don't wait for the provision before you move. God has not promised that you will see it beforehand. You don't try to figure out what God is going to do next and how he will meet your needs; you move forward in the certainty that he is with you, for you, and in you. This God of awesome power will grant you power to do what is needed. This is his sure and reliable covenant promise to you.

And what kind of power does this one to whom you're entrusting your life have? Let me refer you to one of the strangest verses in all of Scripture, one that paints a dramatic picture of the awe-inspiring power of God. It's found in Exodus 11. God is delivering his people from their captivity in Egypt, and all the firstborn of Egypt are going to die, including cattle. God says that as the result of this, there will be a great cry throughout Egypt like there has never been before. Then he says, "But not a dog shall growl against any of the people of Israel, either man or beast, that you may know that the Lord makes a distinction between Egypt and Israel" (v. 7). What kind of power does God have? He has the power to silence the growl of every dog in Egypt. But there is more. He has the power to cause the dogs to distinguish between Israelites and Egyptians. He said the dogs would wail against the Egyptians and be silent in the presence of Israelites, all because there is a God who rules all things. He even has the power to direct individual animals to do what he wants them to do.

Yes, your God has awesome power, distinguishing power. He knows who his people are, he knows where they are, he knows what they need, he knows when they need it, and he knows what needs to be delivered and what needs to be controlled for his will to be done. He always gives the power that his people need.

FOR FURTHER STUDY AND ENCOURAGEMENT
Exodus 6:1–9

DAY 22

*Grace frees you from faking what you don't have
and boasting about what you didn't earn.*

FAKING IS A BIG PART of the culture of fallen humanity. Maybe
you fake it when you tell a story in such a way that it makes
you way more of a hero than you really were when the incident actually happened. Perhaps you fake it when you make
your job seem more important than it really is. Maybe you
fake it when you finagle your way into buying a house that
is way pricier than you can responsibly afford. Maybe you
fake it when you try to work your way into friendships with
people who are far more affluent and positioned than you'll
ever be. Perhaps your fakery is best seen when you act as if
you have much more theological understanding than you
really have or are much more committed to ministry than
you really are. Perhaps you fake it when you present your
marriage as being far more mature and peaceful than it's ever
been. Or maybe you're a fake when you fail to reach out for
help when you are at the end of your rope as a parent. Maybe
your fakery is your unwillingness to confess to the person
next to you that you struggle with the same area of sin that
he or she has just confessed to. Maybe your fakery is in the
big boundary that you have built between your polished
public persona and the messier details of your private life.
Maybe you fake yourself all the time by telling yourself that
you're more righteous than you are.

Here's the question that you need to wrestle with: "Is there someplace or some way in my life where I'm a fake?" Is there someplace where, to yourself or others, you pretend to be something that you're not or where you boast about something you didn't actually do? I think there are artifacts of fakery in all of our lives because there is a desire in all of our hearts to be more independently wise, righteous, and strong than we really are.

"For by grace you have been saved through faith. And this is not your own doing; it is the gift of God, not a result of works, so that no one may boast" (Eph. 2:8–9). Praise God that his grace frees all of his children from their bondage to fakery. Why is this so? God's grace offers you what you did not earn and forgives you for the wrongs you actually did. Grace radically alters your identity and your hope. Your identity is not in what you have achieved or in what the people around you think of what you have achieved. No, as a result of grace, your identity is rooted in the achievements of another. Your hope is not based on how well you are doing, but on what Jesus has done for you. Grace invites you to be real and honest. Grace allows you to live free of false hope and the faux identity of human fakery once and for all, and to rest in the honest and stable identity you have found in Jesus and his eternal work on your behalf.

FOR FURTHER STUDY AND ENCOURAGEMENT
Matthew 6:1–4

DAY 23

*You disobey not because you lack the God-given
grace to obey, but because you love something more
than the God who's given you that grace.*

YOUR DISOBEDIENCE IS NEVER GOD'S FAULT. Maybe you're
thinking: "Of course it's not, Paul. You don't really think that
I think that, do you?" As much as we know theologically that
God is not responsible for our behavior, we have subtle ways
of shifting the blame to him. We say:

- "If only my pastor were more available in times of need,
  then I would've . . ."
- "If only I had had a better job at the time, I wouldn't
  have . . ."
- "If only my parents had been better models for me, I
  could've . . ."
- "If only I had come to Christ earlier in my life, I'm sure
  I would've . . ."
- "If only I hadn't gotten sick, there would've . . ."
- "If only my husband had been more romantic, I wouldn't
  have . . ."
- "If only my children weren't so rebellious, I wouldn't be . . ."
- "If only there weren't so much pornography on the Inter-
  net, I wouldn't have been tempted to . . ."
- "If only I weren't so busy, I could take more time to . . ."

If God is present with you everywhere you go (and he is), and
if he is sovereign over every situation, relationship, and location

of your life (and he is), then when you blame other people for your circumstances or for the wrongs that you do, you are, in fact, blaming God. You are saying that God didn't give you what you needed to be what he has called you to be and to do what he has called you to do. You are essentially saying: "My problem isn't a heart problem; my problem is a *poverty of grace* problem. If only God had given me _____, I wouldn't have had to do what I did." This is the final argument of a self-excusing lifestyle. This argument was first made in the garden of Eden after the rebellion of Adam and Eve. Adam: "The woman you gave me made me do it." Eve: "The devil made me do it." It is the age-old self-defensive lie of a person who doesn't want to face the ugliness of the sin that still resides in his or her heart.

It is hard for us to accept that our words and behavior are not caused by what's outside us, but by what's inside us (see Luke 6:43–45). But the Scriptures are clear that every wrong you and I do flows out of the thoughts and desires of our hearts. It is only when you admit and confess this that you begin to feel the need for and get excited about God's grace. If you have convinced yourself that you're not your problem, but people and situations are, you are not excited about God's provision of powerful forgiving and transforming grace, because, frankly, you don't think you need it. For many of us, subtle patterns of blaming God are in the way of receiving the grace that we need at the very moment we are working to convince ourselves that we don't need it.

FOR FURTHER STUDY AND ENCOURAGEMENT
Deuteronomy 30

DAY 24

*Somehow, some way, your little kingdom will look
very attractive to you today, but it is the very kingdom
from which grace works unrelentingly to rescue you.*

THE BIBLE REALLY IS A STORY OF kingdoms in conflict, and that battle rages on the field of your heart. It rages for control of your soul. The two kingdoms in conflict cannot live in peace with one another. There will never be a truce. There is no safe demilitarized zone where you can live. Each kingdom demands your loyalty and your worship. Each kingdom promises you life. One kingdom leads you to the King of kings and the other sets you up as king. The big kingdom works to dethrone you and decimate your little kingdom of one, while the little kingdom seduces you with promises it cannot deliver. The big kingdom of glory and grace is gorgeous from every perspective, but it doesn't always look that way to you. The little kingdom is deceptive and dark, but at points it appears to you as beautiful and life-giving. You either pray that God's kingdom will come and that his will will be done, or you work to make sure that your will and your way win the day.

So it makes sense that Jesus came to earth as a King to establish his kingdom. Like a heroic monarch, he died so his kingdom would last eternally. But he did not come as an earthly king to set up a physical, political kingdom. He came to set up a much better, much greater, much more expansive kingdom than one that locates itself in a certain place and time. He came to dethrone all other rule and set up his grace-infused, life-giving reign in your heart. He came to free you and me from our bondage to our own self-serving kingdom purposes. He came to help us understand that his grace is not given to make our little kingdom purposes work but to invite us to a much, much better kingdom.

So tell yourself again today that there is a King, but he is not you. Tell yourself that there is a kingdom that will protect and satisfy your heart but it is not yours. As Jesus said, there is a kingdom that you should seek, but you will never, ever be its monarch. Quite apart from anything you could have done, achieved, earned, or deserved, you have been given a kingdom. The price of that gift was the suffering and death of the King. But he conquered death so that by grace he could establish his rule in your heart. Right now he reigns on your behalf (see 1 Cor. 15), and he will continue to do so until the last enemy of your soul and of his kingdom has been defeated. Then he will invite you into the final kingdom, where peace and righteousness will reign forever and ever. This is the story of your faith. The story of this Savior King is now your biography. Why would you ever want to go back to the delusional hopes of your kingdom of one?

FOR FURTHER STUDY AND ENCOURAGEMENT

Exodus 32

DAY 25

*Good is not good enough; complete conformity
to Christ's image is the plan of grace.*

MOST OF US ARE JUST too easily satisfied. It's not that we ask
too much from our Savior. We have the polar opposite problem—we are willing to settle for far too little. Our personal
goals, wishes, and dreams fall far short of God's plans and
purposes for us. God will settle for nothing less than each of
us being completely conformed to the likeness of his Son. He
will finally and completely defeat sin and death. He will not
abandon his purpose for any reason at any time. Our problem
is that often we don't share his mind or buy into his purpose.
Other mentalities capture us:

1. *The Consumer Mentality.* Here we're like religious
   shoppers. We really don't have functional loyalty
   to the plan of God. We're looking for a religious
   experience that is comfortable and meets our felt
   needs, and we have no problem in moving when
   we're dissatisfied.
2. *The "Good Is Good Enough" Mentality.* Here we're thankful for the changes that grace has brought into our lives,
   but we get satisfied too easily. We're satisfied with a little
   bit of biblical literacy or theological knowledge, a slightly
   better marriage, a little personal spiritual growth, and so
   on. We quit seeking, but God is far from being finished
   with transforming us.

3. *The "This Bad Thing Can Work" Mentality.* Here we work to make the best out of what God says is not good. So, for example, a married couple is satisfied with marital détente; they learn to negotiate one another's idolatries rather than working toward a truly godly marriage.

4. *The Personal Comfort vs. Personal Holiness Mentality.* Here what captures our hearts is the craving for a life that is comfortable, pleasurable, predictable, and problem free. We tend to judge God's goodness based on how well life is working for us rather than on his zeal to make good on his redemptive promises to us.

5. *The Event vs. Process Mentality.* Here we are just impatient. We sort of want God to do the good things he has promised us, but we don't want to have to persevere through a lifelong process. We want God's work to be an event rather than a process, and when it's not, our commitment begins to lag.

Ask yourself today, "What do I really want from God?" Have you made the purposes of his grace your life purpose? Do you want what he wants or are you simply too easily satisfied?

FOR FURTHER STUDY AND ENCOURAGEMENT
Philippians 2:1–18

DAY 26

*We wander. God pursues and reconciles. We stumble
and fall. God forgives and restores. We grow tired
and weary. God empowers us by his grace.*

IT IS A HUMBLING AND YET vital thing to acknowledge—you
and I simply don't have much in our relationship with God
and our growth in grace for which we can take credit. The fact
of the matter is that we give daily proof of our ongoing need
for that grace. The reality is that if we followed Jesus for a
thousand years, we would need his grace as much for the next
day as we did the first day that we believed.

He is the sun that gives us light. He is the refuge where
we can hide. He is the water that nourishes us and the bread
that feeds us. He is the solid rock on which we stand. He is
the captain who defends us against the enemy. He is wisdom,
blessing us with the insight of truth. He is the Lamb that bore
the penalty for our sin. He is the high priest who daily brings
our case to the Father. He is the faithful friend who will not
forsake us even in our worst moments. He is the giver who
blesses us with spiritual riches that we could never earn. He is
the one who makes us aware of our sin and brings conviction
to our hearts. He is the shepherd who seeks us when we have
wandered and are lost, and brings us back to the fold of his care.
None of these actions is a luxury for us. They are all necessary
ingredients of our spiritual lives, yet they are not things that
we could ever provide for ourselves. We are like babies, unable

to meet our own needs and completely dependent on the love of our Father for life, sustenance, and health.

Thoughts of independent righteousness are a grand delusion. Taking credit for what only grace can produce is the height of spiritual arrogance. Thinking that the grace you once needed is no longer essential is a recipe for disaster. Without the patience, forgiveness, rescue, provision, transformation, and deliverance of his grace, we would have no spiritual hope whatsoever. We are not spiritually independent in any way. The opposite is true. Just as in the first moment we believed, we are always completely dependent on the grace of the Savior for every spiritual need. We cannot go it on our own. We have not produced fruit by our own righteousness and strength. There really is no good thing that we have that we have not received from God's gracious hand.

So there is no reason to boast. There is nothing for which we can take credit. All praise, honor, worship, and service go to God and God alone. He sought us. He birthed us. He sustains us. He matures us. He protects us. And he will finally deliver us. To him be the glory. Amen.

FOR FURTHER STUDY AND ENCOURAGEMENT

Luke 15:11–32

DAY 27

Yes, change is possible, not because you have
wisdom and strength, but because you've
been blessed with the grace of Jesus.

YOU'RE NOT STUCK. You're not encased in concrete. Your life is not a dead end. The possibility of change has not slipped through your fingers. Change is possible for you and me even in the places where change seems most hopeless. Why? Because the giver of transformative grace has made you and me the place where he dwells!

If you were to ask what God is doing, what he is working on between the "already" of your justification and the "not yet" of your sanctification, the answer could be given in one word: *change.*

First, there is that work of personal growth and change the theologians call progressive sanctification. It is God's lifelong commitment to actually make me what he declared me to be in justification—righteous. In every situation, location, and relationship of my life, God is employing people, places, and things as his tools of transformative grace. He is not resting. He does not leave the work of his hands. He takes no breaks; he is relentlessly working to change me into all that his grace makes it possible for me to be. He will not be content for me to be a little bit better. He will work by grace until I am finally and totally free of sin, that is, molded into the image of his perfectly righteous Son.

This zealous Savior is also a dissatisfied Creator. He is not content to leave this world in its present sin-scarred condition. So there will come a day when he will make all things new. He will return his world to the condition it was in before sin left it so damaged. Change really is the zeal of your Redeemer. Personal change (Titus 2:11–14) and environmental change (Rev. 21:1–5) are his holy zeal. When you are disappointed in yourself, grieved at the sin in your relationships, or upset with the condition of your world and you cry out for change, you are crying for something that hits right at the center of the zeal of your Savior's grace.

Change doesn't mean that you'll get your wish list of things that you think will give you the good life. Change doesn't mean that God will turn the people around you into the people you'd like them to be. And change surely doesn't mean that God will exercise his power to make life easier and more pleasurable according to your definition. But you can rest assured that where real change is needed, there is a God of grace who knows just where that change needs to take place and offers you everything you need so that it can happen.

FOR FURTHER STUDY AND ENCOURAGEMENT

Colossians 3:1–17

DAY 28

It is grace to not be paralyzed by regret.
The cross teaches that you are not stuck,
not cursed to pay forever for your past.

HE SAT BEFORE ME WITH his head in his hands and kept saying over and over again: "I just wish I could have it all back. I just wish I could press a button and do it all over again. I wish I knew then what I know now. I wish I could try again, but I can't." He must have said this or something similar to this ten times. He was incredibly distraught and regretful, and yet in the best spiritual condition he had ever been in. I really did feel his pain and I was very happy that he felt it too, because I knew that what he was experiencing was the pain of grace.

He was a hard, driven, and demanding man who kept moving forward no matter what and never looked back. He didn't care what trail of destruction he left behind him. He was successful. He knew it and wanted everyone else to know it too. He had loved his work more than his family, and in the process, he had lost both. It was all gone—family, job, and wealth. He had played the game by himself and for himself, and had lost in a big way. But now his eyes were open, and the scene broke his heart. Bankrupt and alone, he looked back with grief at every arrogant moment. It was painful, but it was grace. God was making his eyes see so that he would never go back there again.

It's a grace to regret. Grace allows you to face your sin, to own it and not shift the blame. But it is also grace that forgives what has been exposed. Grace forces you to feel the pain of your regrets, but never asks you to pay for them, because the price has already been paid by Jesus. Colossians 2:14 talks about how "the record of debt that stood against us" has been canceled by the sacrifice of Jesus. You can look back, but with your burden lifted by forgiving grace. It is good to look back and celebrate the rescue of grace. It is good to mourn the sins of the past. It is not good to be paralyzed by them. Grace lives at the intersection between clarity of sight and hope for the future. And that grace is yours for the taking. You don't have to rewrite your past, making yourself look more righteous than you ever really were. You can stare the truth in the face because of what Jesus has done for you. You can own what needs to be owned and confess what needs to be confessed, and then move on to live in a new and better way. The same grace that forgives your past empowers you to live in a new way in the future.

So look backward and look forward. God's grace enables you to do both, celebrating forgiveness for the past and embracing power for a new and better future. Only God's grace gifts you with peace with your past and hope for your future.

FOR FURTHER STUDY AND ENCOURAGEMENT
Philippians 3:12–21

DAY 29

You simply must not underestimate sin and
you simply cannot overestimate grace.

THINK FOR A MOMENT: whose sin do you tend to minimize? Your friends'? Your spouse's? Your children's? Your neighbors'? Your extended family members'? Your father's or mother's? Your boss's? For most of us, the problem is not that we underestimate the sin of others. No, we tend to do the opposite. We're typically all too focused on the failure of others. We find it all too easy to point out their flaws. We're all tempted to keep a running record of the specific sins of the people around us. If we were honest, most of us would have to humbly confess that we tend to be far more concerned about the sin of the people around us than our own. We tend to be hyperaware of the weaknesses of those living near us while we appear to be functionally blind to our own. For this reason, we begin to forget that we are more like them than unlike them, that there are few things that we can see in the lives of others that are not present in our own lives in some way.

Now, this outward concern/inward denial dynamic is not okay. Blindness to your own sin is a denial of the presence of personal spiritual need. Such a denial always leads to a devaluing of and a resistance to God's grace. Denying your need for grace and underestimating the power of what that grace can do never, ever leads to anything good.

Here's the problem—this side of forever, we are all very good at doing both. We're all very good at looking at our sin and naming it less than sin, and we all tend to degrade the glory of what grace has done, is doing, and will do. People who deny sin tend to not progressively conquer it, and people who devalue grace tend not to run to it for help. What we're talking about here are the two sides of a healthy Christian life. You confess that although you are in Christ, the presence of sin is still within you. However, it is being progressively defeated, and you humbly embrace the fact that you have been given glorious grace that can do for you what you could never do for yourself.

The admission of sin doesn't lead you somewhere dark and depressing, because you know you've been given grace that is greater than your sin, and your celebration of grace is real and heartfelt because it's done in the context of your confession of the very sin that grace addresses. Confession of sin without the celebration of grace leads to guilt, self-loathing, timidity, and spiritual paralysis. Embracing grace without the admission of sin leads to confident theological "always rightism," but does not result in change in your heart and life. So today, refuse to minimize sin, reject the temptation to devalue grace, and run to Jesus weeping and celebrating at the same time.

FOR FURTHER STUDY AND ENCOURAGEMENT

1 John 2:1–17

DAY 30

We disobey. God convicts and restores. We doubt.
God works to make us people of faith. We hunger.
God feeds us with the bounty of his grace.

Plenteous grace
is what we're given;
grace that is
deeper,
fuller,
richer,
and greater
than our sin.
This grace does not
suspend operations
in the face of our
disobedience.
It will not
turn its back
in the face of our
doubt.
It will not stand
idly by
in the face of our
hunger.

No, this is
rich grace,
perseverant grace,
tender grace,
powerful grace.
There really is nothing
like it,
because it comes from the hand
of Jesus.

FOR FURTHER STUDY AND ENCOURAGEMENT

1 Timothy 1:12–17

DAY 31

We're all still a bit of a mess; that's why
we need God's grace today as much as we
needed it the first day we believed.

YOU AND I NEED TO SAY IT to ourselves again and again. We need to look in the mirror and make the confession as part of our morning routine. Here's what we all need to say: "I am not a grace graduate."

It is so tempting to mount arguments for your own righteousness:

- "That really wasn't lust. I'm just a man who enjoys beauty."
- "That really wasn't gossip. It was just a very detailed, very personal prayer request."
- "I wasn't angry at my kids. I was just acting as one of God's prophets. 'Thus says the Lord . . .'"
- "I'm not on an ugly quest for personal power. No, I'm just exercising God-given leadership gifts."
- "I'm not coldhearted and stingy. I'm just trying to be a good steward of what God has given me."
- "I wasn't being proud. I just thought someone needed to take control of the conversation."
- "It wasn't really a lie. It was just a different way of recounting the facts."

We all tend to want to think we are more righteous than we actually are. We don't like to think of ourselves as still desperately in need of God's rescuing grace. And we surely don't want to face the fact that what we need to be rescued from is us! When you argue for your own righteousness, working hard to deny the empirical evidence of your sin, then you fail to seek the amazing grace that is your only hope. Grace is only ever attractive to sinners. The riches of God's goodness are only ever sought by the poor. The spiritual healing of the Great Physician is only ever esteemed by those who acknowledge that they still suffer from the spiritual disease of sin. It's a tragedy when we praise God for his grace on Sunday and deny our need for that grace the rest of the week. Face the fact today that you'll never outgrow your need for grace, no matter how much you learn and how much you mature, until you are on the other side and your struggle is over because sin is no more (see Phil. 3:12–16). The way to begin to celebrate the grace that God so freely gives you every day is by admitting how much you need it.

FOR FURTHER STUDY AND ENCOURAGEMENT
Psalm 32

DAY 32

*Since God writes your story, he knows what you're facing
and exactly what grace you'll need to live his way.*

ADMIT IT: YOUR LIFE HASN'T worked out according to your
plan. Last month didn't work out according to your plan.
Today won't work out according to your plan. All of this is true
because you aren't the author of your story. You don't need to
read a mystery novel; your life is a mystery to you. You and I
don't have a clue what is around the next corner, let alone where
we will be and what we will be doing a decade from now. But
even though there is very little that we know for sure about
our lives and we experience constant surprises along the way,
we need not give way to panic. Yes, our lives are out of our
control, but that doesn't mean they are out of control. No, our
lives are under the careful administration of the one who had
the wisdom and power to be the great Author of it all.

Since God is the Author of every detail of your story, since
he writes into your story every situation, location, and relationship, then he knows exactly what you're facing and precisely
what grace you need to face it in the way he has planned. You
could say it this way: his sovereign control is the guarantee
that you will have everything that he has promised you. His
sovereign control means he knows what you need because he
has planned for you everything that you're now facing. But
more needs to be said. His sovereignty is your surety because he
can guarantee the delivery of his promises only in the location

where he rules. Because he rules over all things at all times (since he wrote the story that includes it all), he can guarantee that you and I will have what he has promised us in the places and at the times they are needed.

Paul says it this way: "And he made from one man every nation of mankind to live on all the face of the earth, having determined allotted periods and the boundaries of their dwelling place, that they should seek God, and perhaps feel their way toward him and find him. Yet he is actually not far from each one of us" (Acts 17:26–27). Paul doesn't think of God as an "out-there and distant sovereign." He reminds us that because God is involved with every detail of our lives, he is near. He is so near that at any moment we can reach out and touch him. This means that every grace that you and I will ever need is near and available to us as well. So reach out today. The Author is near and he has grace in his hands.

FOR FURTHER STUDY AND ENCOURAGEMENT

1 Peter 1:13–25

DAY 33

You were created to be dependent.
God welcomes your dependency with his grace,
so why would you want to go it on your own?

WRAPPED INTO THE DEVIOUS TEMPTATION of the serpent in the garden were two foundational lies. These lies have been believed somehow, some way by every person who has ever lived. If you're a parent, you've seen the acceptance of them in your children from a very early age.

The first lie is the lie of *autonomy*. This lie tells you that you are an independent human, that your life belongs to you, and that you have the right to live your life as you please. It is an attractive and seductive lie. Believing this lie makes a little child protest when he's told to go to bed or to eat his peas. However, the doctrine of creation destroys the lie of autonomy. Think with me. Creation depicts ownership. I am a painter by avocation. Once I have composed, painted, and completed a painting, it belongs to me because I made it. You can buy it from me or I can gift it to you, but until I relinquish it, it is mine because I created it. Since God created you and me, we belong to him. We don't own our mentality, our spirituality, our emotionality, our psychology, our personality, or our physicality. We are not independent beings and we do not have a natural right to do with our physical and spiritual selves whatever we desire to do. Autonomy is a life-destroying lie.

The second lie is the lie of *self-sufficiency.* This lie tells you that you have everything within yourself to be what you're supposed to be and to do what you're supposed to do. This lie explains why a little child struggling to tie his shoelaces will slap his mom's hand away when she tries to help, even though he has no idea how to make a bow. However, the doctrine of creation destroys this lie as well. Creation depicts dependency. The flower you plant in your garden is not self-sufficient. If it is not weeded and not watered, it will not grow. You and I were created to be dependent, first on God and second on others in interdependent relationships. Immediately after creating Adam and Eve, God began to talk to them because he knew they had no capacity to figure life out on their own. The lie of self-sufficiency is also life-destroying because it causes us to resist the help of our Creator—the very help we were designed to need and he is willing to give.

Going it on your own simply does not work. The self-made man is always poorly made. Here is an argument for how much we need grace. It takes an act of grace to release us from our bondage to these lies so that we will confess our need for grace and then seek the grace that is our only hope in life and death. It really does take grace to know how much you need grace.

FOR FURTHER STUDY AND ENCOURAGEMENT
John 15:1–17

DAY 34

*Even pleasure preaches grace. Every day we
all experience a symphony of pleasures we
never could've earned the right to enjoy.*

THESE ARE SOME OF God's pleasant gifts to us:

- the sound of the birds in the spring
- the delicate beauty of a rose
- the multihued display of a sunset
- the pristine blanket of new-fallen snow
- the tenderness of a kiss
- the smell of flowers in bloom
- the wide variety of tastes and textures of food
- the glory of a wonderful piece of music
- the bright colors of leaves in the fall
- the enjoyment of a great drama
- the wonder of a master's painting
- the sweet voice of a child
- the stunning grandeur of a mountain

God created for us a world of amazing beauty where pleasures exist all around us. He created us with pleasure gates (eyes,
ears, mouths, noses, hands, brains, and so on) so that we could
take in the pleasure. He blesses us with these good and beautiful
things every day. That means that on your very worst day and
on your very best day, you are blessed with pleasures that come
right from the hand of God. That tells you that you don't get

these pleasures because you've earned or deserved them, but because he is a God of grace. He graces you with good things because he is good, not because you are.

Perhaps it's just a really good sandwich at lunch. You don't deserve the pleasure of that sandwich. You don't deserve a tongue that can take in its tastes and textures. You don't deserve a brain that can make sense of the whole experience. It is just another gift from the hands of God, who daily bestows on you what you do not deserve because he loves you. Maybe you look out your window and see that the leaves on your tree have turned fire red. The sight takes your breath away. Stop and be thankful that the God of amazing grace created that tree and your ability to see, understand, and enjoy it. He chose you to experience its pleasure at that moment because he is the God of tender, patient grace: "For he makes his sun rise on the evil and on the good, and sends rain on the just and on the unjust" (Matt. 5:45).

FOR FURTHER STUDY AND ENCOURAGEMENT

Psalm 104

DAY 35

*The transformative power of grace will be one
of the divine wonders that we will celebrate
forever when eternity is our final home.*

THE BIBLE IS NOT a collection of stories of human heroes. No,
the Bible is the story of a hero Redeemer who transforms weak
and ordinary people by his powerful grace. Think with me of
the characters who walk across the pages of Scripture:

- Moses wasn't a natural-born leader. He begged God to
  send someone else to Egypt, yet by transforming grace,
  there was no prophet in all of Israel like him.
- Joshua was scared to death of what God was calling him
  to do, but by divine power, he led the Israelites into the
  promised land.
- Gideon was convinced God had the wrong address, that he
  didn't really mean to call Gideon to lead the Israelite army
  against the Midianites, but when Gideon did it, he wit-
  nessed the awesome power of the God who had called him.
- Samson forsook his calling for the love of a deceitful
  woman, but he brought down the temple of Dagon by
  the power of God.
- David was the least likely son of Jesse to rise to the throne
  of Israel, but God's grace gave him a heart of courage.
- Elijah, when left to himself in a moment of discourage-
  ment, asked God to take his life, but he did great things
  by God's power.

- Peter was so fearful that he denied that he knew Jesus, but he became the man who stood before the Sanhedrin and essentially said, "You can threaten to kill me, but I will not stop preaching the gospel" (see Acts 4:19–20).
- Paul was the least likely of the apostles. He had murderous hatred for the followers of Jesus, yet by grace he became the most eloquent spokesman of the gospel.

The Bible does not celebrate the steely spirit of a bunch of heroic characters. No, the Bible puts before us people who were just like you and me. They were weak and fearful. They were easily deceived and disloyal. They doubted God as much as they trusted him. They sometimes followed God's way and at other times demanded their own way. These were not natural-born heroes. These were not individuals to be celebrated. Yet, they all accomplished great things, things that were crucial for the advancement of God's purpose. What made the difference? You can answer the question with one word: grace. Grace transformed their hearts, giving them the desire, power, and wisdom to do what they would not have been able to do on their own. Grace means that when God calls you, he goes with you, supplying what you need for the task at hand. They weren't naturals; no, they were transformed!

FOR FURTHER STUDY AND ENCOURAGEMENT

Revelation 19

(Listen to what the voices on the other side celebrate.)

DAY 36

*Today you will celebrate that grace has made
you part of God's great plan or mourn the places
where you aren't getting your own way.*

HE MAY HAVE BEEN the hardest person I ever counseled. He was
self-assured and controlling. He argued for the rightfulness of
everything he had ever done. He acted like the victim when
in fact he was the victimizer. He had crushed his marriage and
alienated his children. He loved himself and had a wonderful plan for his life. It was his will in his way at his time. He
made everyone a slave to his plan or he drove them out of his
life. He made incredible sacrifices to get what he wanted but
chafed against the sacrifices God called him to make. But in a
moment of grace I will never forget, he quit fighting, controlling, and defending. He asked me to stop talking and said:
"Paul, I get it. I have been so busy being God that I have had
little time or interest in serving God." It was one of the most
accurate moments of self-diagnosis I had ever experienced. He
was right. No sooner had the words come out of his mouth
than he began to weep like I had never seen a man weep. His
body shook with grief as grace began its work of freeing him
from his bondage to himself.

But my friend was not unique. If you're a parent, you know
that your children are collections of self-sovereignty. All a child
really wants is his own way. He doesn't want to be told what
to eat, what to wear, when to go to bed, how to steward his

possessions, or how to treat others. He wants to be in the center of his own little world and to write his own set of rules. And he is surprised that you have the audacity to tell him what to do. But it isn't just children. Sin causes this self-sovereignty to live in all of us. We tend to want more control than we are wise enough or strong enough to handle. We want people to follow our way and stay out of our way. But when we wish for these things, we are forgetting who we are, who God is, and what grace has blessed us with. We are always either mourning the fact that we aren't getting our way or celebrating that grace welcomes us to a new and better way. We are either frustrated that we lack control or resting in the one who is "head over all things to the church" (Eph. 1:22). I think there is probably a mix of mourning and celebration in all of us.

What will it be for you today? Will you give way to the frustration that you are not getting your way or celebrate the grace that has included you in the most wonderful plan that was ever conceived?

FOR FURTHER STUDY AND ENCOURAGEMENT
Psalm 73

DAY 37

Today you'll envy the blessings of another or you'll bask in the wonder of the amazing grace you have been given.

I WISH I COULD SAY that I am always content. I wish I could say that I never complain. I wish I could say that I never want what others have. I wish I could say that I have never envied the life of another. I wish I could say that I have never thought that God gave something to someone else that he meant for me. I wish I could say that I am better at counting my blessings than I am at assessing what I don't have. I wish I could say that my appetite for things wasn't so large. I wish my heart would finally be satisfied. These are all wishes because they are not yet completely true of me. Envy still lurks in my heart. It is one of the dark results of the sin that still resides there.

Why does the Bible speak so strongly against envy? Here it is: when envy rules your heart, the love of God doesn't. Let's think about what envy does. It assumes that you deserve blessings that you don't deserve. When your heart is ruled by envy, the attitude of "I am blessed" gets replaced with the attitude of "I deserve." Envy is selfish to the core. Envy always puts you in the center of the world. It makes everything all about you. It causes you to examine life from the sole perspective of your wants, needs, and feelings.

Sadly, envy causes you to question the goodness, faithfulness, and wisdom of God. Envy accuses God of not knowing what he's doing or of not being faithful to what he's promised to do.

When you are convinced that a blessing that another person has ought to belong to you, you don't just have a problem with that person, you have a problem with God. When you begin to question God's goodness, you quit going to him for help. Why? Because you don't seek the help of someone you've come to doubt.

Envy does something else that is spiritually deadly. It assumes understanding that no one has. Envy not only assumes that you know more about that other person's life than you could ever know, it assumes that you have a clearer understanding of what is best than God does. Furthermore, envy causes you to forget God's amazing rescuing, transforming, empowering, and delivering grace. You become so occupied with accounting for what you do not have that the enormous blessings of God's grace—blessings that we could not have earned, achieved, or deserved—go unrecognized and uncelebrated. And because envy focuses more on what you want than it does on the life that God has called you to, it keeps you from paying attention to God's commands and warnings, and therefore leaves you in moral danger.

The only solution to envy is God's rescuing grace—grace that turns self-centered sinners into joyful and contented worshipers of God.

FOR FURTHER STUDY AND ENCOURAGEMENT
1 Samuel 12

DAY 38

*Every time you desire to do and choose to
do what is right in God's eyes, you celebrate
the grace that is yours in Christ Jesus.*

IT'S HARD TO ADMIT, but doing what is right isn't natural for us. Sin turns us all into self-appointed sovereigns over our own little kingdoms. Sin makes us all self-absorbed and self-focused. Sin causes us all to name ourselves righteous. Sin seduces us into thinking we are somehow, some way smarter than God. Sin causes us all to trust in our own wisdom. Sin makes us all want to write our own rules. Sin makes us resistant to criticism and change. Sin makes our eyes and our hearts wander. Sin causes us to crave material things more than spiritual provision. Sin causes us to want and esteem pleasure more than character. In our quest to be God, sin causes us to forget God. It reduces us all to glory thieves, taking for ourselves the glory that belongs to him. All of this means that sin causes us to step over God's wise boundaries in thought, desire, word, and action again and again. This is what's natural for a sinner.

So when you have a hunger to know what is right in God's eyes, when you care about his glory, when you willingly submit to his will, when you forsake your plan for his plan, and when you find joy in surrendering to his lordship, you know that you have been visited by rescuing grace. Notice how Paul talks about our submission to the will of the Father: "Therefore, my beloved, as you have always obeyed, so now, not only as in my presence but much more in my absence, work out your own salvation with fear and trembling, for it is God who works in you, both to will and to work for his good pleasure" (Phil. 2:12–13).

Here is a call to a faith-filled life of submission and obedience. It is a call to be serious about the life that grace has made possible for you. The passage is a call to follow the example of the Lord Jesus Christ. But then Paul reminds you that if you follow, if you obey, and if you do what is right in the eyes of your Savior, you can take no credit whatsoever. This is because your right desires and your right actions exist only because of his indwelling presence and ever-active grace. Paul is saying that we do the right that we do because grace is at that moment rescuing us from ourselves. Grace is protecting us from the self-righteousness and self-sovereignty that would make us all too independent and all too rebellious.

Every moment of our obedience is an evidence of and a celebration of the grace that not only forgives but rescues, and not only rescues but transforms. We live in God's sight not in our own strength, but only by grace.

FOR FURTHER STUDY AND ENCOURAGEMENT
Romans 6:15–23

DAY 39

*If you look into the mirror of God's word and
see someone in need of grace, why would you be
impatient with others who share that need?*

MAYBE ONE OF THE BIGGEST sins in our relationships with one another is the sin of forgetting. I wish I could say that this is not my problem, but it is. It is so easy to forget how profound your need of grace is, and it is equally easy to forget the amazing grace that has been freely showered upon you. And when you forget the grace that you've been given, it becomes very easy to respond to the people around you with nongrace.

It is very clear that grace toward others isn't best born out of duty. Pretend with me that I plop down on the couch next to my dear wife, Luella, and say these words: "You know, Luella, I have come to the realization that it's my duty to be gracious to you. So I'll tell you what I'm going to do. I'm going to give you grace, not because I really want to, but because I guess it's what I have to do." Do you think that Luella would be encouraged by that statement for a moment? I think not. A joyful life of grace toward others grows best in the soil of gratitude. When I really reflect on who I am, when I take time to consider the grace that I couldn't have earned, achieved, or deserved but which has been lavished on me, and when I remember that that grace came at the cost of the life of another, then I am joyfully motivated to give that grace to others.

For the believer, harsh, critical, impatient, and irritated responses to others are always connected to forgetting or denying who we are and what we have been given in Jesus. It is very clear that no one gives grace better than a person who is deeply convinced of his own need of it and who is cogently aware of the grace he has been, and is being, given.

Because we forget so quickly, because we fall into believing that we are deserving, and because we tend to think that we're more righteous and capable than we actually are, we all need to be given grace right at the very moment when we are called to be a tool of grace in the life of another. The God of grace is working his grace into everyone in the room. First John 4:19 really is true: "We love because he first loved us." Now, that's worth remembering.

FOR FURTHER STUDY AND ENCOURAGEMENT
Ephesians 3:14–21

DAY 40

*God is not satisfied with you being a witness
to his work of grace. He's called you to be
an instrument of that grace to others.*

THE POSITION GOD HAS CHOSEN for us in the work of his kingdom is an amazing thing. All of his children have a mind-boggling calling. Sadly, many of them don't understand their position, and because they don't, they are quite comfortable being consumers and quite timid when it comes to being instruments.

So many people who attend evangelical churches on Sunday have little life commitment to the work of those churches. Most pastors would be thrilled if the vast majority of their people were every-Sunday attenders and committed to financially supporting the work of the churches. But all this sadly falls far below God's wise design for his church. Think about it: you will simply never be able to hire enough professional ministry people to cover all the ministry needs in a given week, no matter what size your church is. It is no wonder people reach outside the body of Christ for help. It is no wonder problems are left to grow until they reach intense levels of complication.

All God's children have been called to the same position. We've all been called to be his ambassadors. Remember, the only thing an ambassador does is represent. God's plan is to make his invisible presence and his invisible grace visible through his people, who incarnate his presence and carry that grace to others. That's God's call to every one of his children. There are to be no self-satisfied recipients, no consumers. The body of Christ is designed by God to be an organic, constantly ministering community.

If the church is ever going to be this, then God's people need three things. First, we need *vision*. We need to be reminded again and again of our place in the work of the Redeemer. Next, we need *commitment*. We need to be encouraged to make specific and concrete decisions to better position ourselves for the work to which God has called us. Last, we need *training*. We need to understand what it really looks like to represent the grace of the Redeemer in the lives of the people whom he puts in our paths. We need to be trained not to see those relationships as belonging to us for our happiness, but rather as workrooms in which the Lord can do his transforming work of grace.

What an amazing way to live! We have been chosen by God to be part of the most important work of the universe. We have been chosen to carry the life-changing message of the grace of the Savior King with us wherever we go. And we have been given the same grace to enable us to be the ambassadors that we have been chosen to be.

FOR FURTHER STUDY AND ENCOURAGEMENT
1 Chronicles 16:8–27

SCRIPTURE INDEX

PAUL TRIPP MINISTRIES

Paul Tripp Ministries is a not-for-profit organization connecting the transforming power of Jesus Christ to everyday life. Hundreds of resources are freely available online, on social media, and the Paul Tripp app.

PaulTripp.com

 /pdtripp   @paultripp  @paultrippquotes

More Devotionals
from Paul David Tripp

For more information, visit **crossway.org, paultripp.com,**
or anywhere Christian books are sold.